Kids ministry, kids ministry is where I feel most called. Last year at camp I had no clue where I was called, when people asked me I had absolutly no clue. When I came last year I kept asking God, praying about my calling, and one day it hit me, that I wanted to teach kids about Jesus, and make them see how powerful he truly is. I used to think I was never going to get called into ministry, and it made me upset. So I prayed and asked God everyday, and when the time was right, I knew kids ministry was for me Every chance I get I go help in the nursery at my church, the more I go the more God is telling me that's where I belong. Now I'm here at called camp, still knowing I'm called for kids ministry. And I'm thankful God has shown me my calling.

— CALLED CAMP/2025 ——— BW

Other Works by Tim Barker

CALLED CAMP
—— 2025 —

CALLED CAMP
—— 2025 ——

TIM R. BARKER, D. MIN.

NETWORK PASTOR/SUPERINTENDENT
SOUTH TEXAS MINISTRY NETWORK

CALLED CAMP 2025, Barker, Tim.

1st ed.

ISBN: 979-8-9924875-1-0

DEDICATION

From the moment the idea of Called Camp was introduced to the Network Executive Presbytery, it received overwhelming support. Our dedicated leaders not only embraced the vision but also provided financial backing for the event. Pastors Mike Allard, Don Wiehe, Deborah Prihoda, and Doug Roberts, along with Drs. Jim Rion, John Aniemeke, and Dolly Thomas, are committed to investing in the next generation.

Tim R. Barker

Contents

INTRODUCTION

Today is our day to choose.

Yes, you read that right. It's time for US to choose whether we are willing to do God's work or not.

God has *already chosen us*.

That's what Called Camp is all about, bringing that knowledge to our youth, to teach them to recognize how to know the Call of the Lord and *then to move into it*.

We often think that to be called, we need to lead a revival or be the soloist in the church choir. David, who would one day be the King of Israel, was a shepherd! Jesus started as a babe in a manger. It took Him 33 years to begin His ministry. *33 years!* How many of us are willing to wait that long before seeing God move in our life?

Poor Noah. How did he manage? It took him 100 YEARS to scrabble the ark together. Modern day Christians would have called it quits about six weeks in!

Here's the point: Our youth need to know that the Call starts out with small things. When I was young, I cleaned the church … that's the beginning of my ministry! I got paid, but it was still mopping floors and cleaning up other people's messes.

The message we can share with our youth starts with encouragement and support as they begin testing out their Call. We can chauffeur them as they volunteer, provide snacks when necessary, and allow them to occasionally mess up and start over.

It seems one of the disciples did just that. You will remember that the rooster did crow three times.

Our youth need us. After all, they WILL BECOME the church of tomorrow, and their training starts TODAY!

GOD CALLS US!

I want you to look around and consider with me that GOD CALLS PEOPLE LIKE US! You may be thinking *... I see it in that person ... or this person* .... but in reality, this is a UNIQUE BUNCH here this weekend!

This is what I want you to understand: GOD CALLS US!

Our Network Executive Presbyters all have very unique callings. You may recognize their names ... or maybe not ... either way ... listen to their unique stories ...

DR. DOLLY THOMAS

As a child, I had a sense that God wanted to do something *more* with the life He had given me. My first stirring occurred during tragedy, when my father was killed in a car accident that involved my whole family.

While in a shared hospital room, they told my little seven-year-old brother that Dad had died, and Tobin let out a piercing scream. At that moment, the Lord did something. While in my own pain, He allowed me to hurt deeply for my brother's loss. God birthed something in me: compassion, a call to help the brokenhearted.

Fast forward many years, I was in graduate school for clinical psychology and thought that was it—I was going to be a counselor, but God showed me the greater mission He had in mind. While on a two-month mission trip to India before completing my PhD, I met a missionary who introduced me to biblical counseling, and God showed me a particular Scripture everywhere I went, even in a predominantly Hindu area. "The harvest is plenty, but the laborers are few" (Matt. 9:37). God was making it clear that He was calling me to minister to the brokenhearted, not just with education and knowledge, but through the Word of God and through the power of the Holy Spirit.

God put on my heart that I needed a life partner who was just as committed to ministry, and He answered my prayers in giving me a godly husband. George and I got connected with Teen Challenge shortly after we married, and it's been an amazing journey of a step-by-step leading of one door opening just in time for the next leg of the journey. Over the years, God has used both my education and tragedy in various settings to teach at Evangel University; start my own biblical counseling practice; share the message of hope and healing in several mission fields; and serve at Adult & Teen Challenge of Texas, overseeing counseling and training. Today, it's a joy to serve our Network leadership and participate in the National Mental Health Committee of the AG. I see daily how God can take a life that is yielded to Him and make something beautiful out of our ashes, out of our brokenness, out of our education and inclinations, and out of our YES to Him. To God be all the glory! CALLED CAMP —2025—

PASTOR DEBORAH PRIHODA

Although I can pinpoint the moment in time where I first sensed God's call into ministry, I've come to realize that His Call has been more of an ongoing journey rather than a one-moment encounter. I've had to be willing to continually cultivate an attitude of "Yes, Lord," especially when the Lord has challenged me to trust Him in the midst of insecurity and trepidation. You see, one thing I know for certain is that when God calls us into ministry, He isn't looking on our resume at our qualifications, but He's searching out areas of our lives where we feel the most vulnerable. WHY? 2 Corinthians 12:9 best answers this question: "*My grace is all you need. My power works best in weakness.*" So now I am glad to boast about my weaknesses, so that the power of Christ can work through me.

I have had some wonderful and amazing doors of opportunity opened for me in the ministry of which I am so very grateful. *God's Call* into ministry, which began as an unassuming dramatic script, has grown and changed through the years to allow me additional opportunities to teach, pastor, mentor, minister in disasters, as well as serve in leadership opportunities. My journey has definitely been exciting thus far! I can say without hesitation that I look forward to the road ahead with great expectation … and just to think it all began with and will continue as long as I am willing to simply say, "Yes, Lord." CALLED CAMP
————2025—

DR. JOHN ANIEMEKE

Born into a clergy home of six children, we were all involved in some type of church-related ministry. I discovered that after giving my life to Christ at six years old, my love and passion for God increased more and more like the boy Samuel in the Bible.

Honestly speaking, I didn't really know that one day I would be called into pastoral ministry, but I sensed a deep passion for God all through my years growing up and while in college. I was tested and involved in multiple areas of ministry (almost like mini-internships) in various roles in the Royal Rangers, children's ministry, Christ's Ambassadors (CA), youth ministries, Chi Alpha, choir, choir director, drama, deacon, associate pastor and more. And yet, while I wanted to do more for God, at that time, in the place I was serving, there was a glass ceiling I could not break through. It became a wilderness experience for me. It was while seeking God to break the glass ceiling that my Call came for the next assignment into pastoral ministry with clear instructions to go back to the Assemblies of God and plant a church where people of all nations and tribes could come and worship the Lord as one people. The mandate was to ignite revival and stir up many to serve the Lord as well.

We started with eight people in my little living room, and it was all by faith. We did not know what was next, where the people would come from, or much of anything but to seek more of God. I can boldly say my continued obedience has and continues to pay off, because I keep seeing God making a way where there seems to be no way.

Bethel Covenant has grown and continues to grow, not by might, nor by power, but by the Spirit of God, and I am glad I obeyed God's call at the age of 33. Most importantly, I am glad God prepared me well and captured my heart early; and I pray that I will continue to love and serve Him all the days of my life.

I gladly encourage anyone who is scared of what the future holds that when you walk in obedience, you will discover the best of God. I trust God with my life because He is the faithful who has called us, and if you place your trust in Him, He will be faithful to you just as He has been to me. CALLED CAMP
—2025—

PASTOR DON WIEHE

I was saved in the summer of 1975, the summer after my junior year in high school. From that moment, I had an overwhelming desire to serve the Lord and His Church. Such joy and fulfillment came as I shared my faith, won my friends to the Lord, and served in various capacities within the church. I just served where needed. It really didn't matter what I did, I just enjoyed serving. At each stage of my calling into ministry, it was a combination of having peace with God and a confirming word from those within the Body of Christ. God used others to encourage me in my calling with an encouraging statement here, an idea shared there, and an invitation to serve. It's hard to believe, but this coming July 2025 will be 50 years of walking with the Lord and serving His Church. CALLED CAMP —2025—

PASTOR MIKE ALLARD

As I reflect on my faith journey, I want to share a profound night that changed my life forever.

It was December 31st, 1973, when I attended a watch night service at Evangel Temple Assembly of God in

Wichita Falls where Brother Carl Alcorn was the pastor. The guest evangelist that evening was Mike Evans, a Messianic Jew. Although it wasn't my home church, I felt compelled to go since they were "praying in the New Year." My friend, Robert Hogue, who was a few years older, took his car. It was a powerful evening of worship, prayer, and preaching.

Mike Evans spoke with incredible anointing that night. When he gave the altar call, I couldn't wait to go forward. To be honest, I don't recall the message or even the topic. I had accepted Christ when I was eleven, and that fall, Robert and I were both baptized in the Holy Spirit. This night felt like another level of spiritual awakening. God began to speak to me in a profound way, as if He were downloading powerful truths into my heart. I remember being slain under the power of the Holy Spirit, overwhelmed by His presence. One moment I was standing; the next, I found myself on the ground, worshiping the Lord. I couldn't tell you how long I stayed there, but it felt timeless. It was not just a brief experience but a glorious and powerful touch from heaven. I recall speaking in tongues for a long time, and I didn't want it to end. When I left the service that night, I felt over-whelmed, in the best way possible, by the presence of the Lord.

Around two am the following morning, I returned home. My relationship with my mom was wonderful, especially since my dad wasn't home that night. I loved my dad deeply; he had been a pastor but was backslidden and running from the Lord while working as a crop duster. He would sometimes be gone for months without a word, leaving us in a depressing silence that often felt like abandonment. This absence contributed to my desire for a strong home and a faithful father.

When I got home, my mom woke up, and we talked for a long while. She had an amazing way of recognizing God's presence in my life. I shared everything that had happened that night, and I asked her where I should start reading in my Bible. She suggested 1 Samuel, mentioning that I had expressed interest in David.

That night, I read the first chapter of 1 Samuel and thought, "Wow, I'm really doing well!" I closed my Bible, feeling proud of myself. Then, I felt the Lord urging me, "Read another chapter." As I read the next chapter, one verse jumped out at me:

> *"Then I will raise up for Myself a faithful priest*
> *who shall do according to what is in My heart*
> *and in My mind. I will build him a sure house,*
> *and he shall walk before My anointed forever."*
> 1 Samuel 2:35 NKJV

As I read those words, the Lord spoke to my heart saying, "That's you! You will be My faithful priest. You'll do all that which is in My heart and mind, and I will build you a sure house; you shall walk before My anointed forever."

I was overwhelmed with joy in that moment, forgetting how late it was, and ran back to tell my mom. She was so happy for me, and that night I accepted the call of God on my life.

Now, after fifty years of following Him, I look back fondly on the journey. I preached my first sermon in April 1974 at Northwest Assembly of God in Wichita Falls. It's been a great privilege to travel around the world and tell people about Christ. I've led thousands in the sinner's prayer, baptized many, and stood before countless people proclaiming Jesus as Lord and Savior. I am grateful for the life I've had.

I married an incredible woman 45 years ago, and together we have three wonderful children, who have married the best spouses. They've blessed us with twelve grandchildren. I've served as a kid's pastor, youth pastor, district youth director, and now as a lead pastor. Life has had its ups and downs, but through it all, it has been the greatest adventure.

If I could go back in time and someone offered me a button to press to relive it all, I would press it in a heartbeat!

Thank you for asking about the call of God on my life. It has truly been the greatest joy of my life to serve Jesus and His church. CALLED CAMP —2025—

PASTOR DOUG ROBERTS

My call would not be described as hearing an audible voice of God. It would be more accurately described as obedience to doors of opportunity. When my wife, Janet, and I were a very young married couple, the Sunday school superintendent at Peoria First Assembly asked us to take the Jr. High ministry. We were nineteen at the time and assumed they were making a huge mistake or had simply been turned down by all of the qualified people. We respectfully declined. They asked a second time. Again, we respectfully declined. Then they asked us a third time, and we were too embarrassed to decline again, because it would make us look so unspiritual. We tried it ... and we loved it. We loved the kids, and they seemed to love us. God was showing us that we actually had something to offer for His kingdom despite the mistakes that we had made in our dating relationship. After two years of working with the Jr. High ministry, we moved to San Antonio. We were almost immediately asked to teach the Jr. High Sunday school class. We happily accepted and within a year we were asked to become the youth pastors.

We were youth pastors at Faith Assembly for almost ten years while also working full time jobs outside the church. I was also the church drummer. On a Monday morning at work, I received a call from the senior pastor informing me that he would like for me to lead praise and worship the following Sunday. I said it would be awkward leading from the drums. He said, "No, you'll lead from the keyboard."

I told him that I don't really play keyboards, and he said, "Well, you've got until Sunday to learn how!"

I seriously considered declining this offer, but I just couldn't shake what I felt God was saying to me. "I've never asked you to do anything that you weren't capable of doing."

So, even though this was certainly the scariest thing that I had ever been asked to do, I agreed to lead worship. Thankfully, there are no early recordings of this, but just as God promised, I found that not only did I enjoy it, but God continued to enable me and increase my abilities on keyboards. He was teaching me to learn how to lead a congregation in worship.

After being obedient to walking through that door of ministry, I can assuredly say that it was music ministry that would open up all the future doors of ministry to me. I was offered the position of music minister back at Peoria First Assembly. After two years, I was offered the position of music minister and associate pastor at Calvary

Temple in San Antonio. I still didn't really envision myself as a senior pastor, but after three years I was asked to let my name be voted on as Senior Pastor. We were elected with a 99 percent vote. Twenty-five years later, my wife and I are still the senior pastors here, and I've had the privilege of serving in the section presbytery for ten years and now serve as an executive presbyter.

God will never open a door of ministry where He doesn't already know that you'll be successful and used mightily in His kingdom.

It all starts with obedience. CALLED CAMP ————2025—

DR. JIM RION

I was saved at a youth camp at age fourteen. It would take me about two years to fully realize I was called into full-time ministry. Looking back, I believe my Call came at the time I was saved. My conversion was an Acts 9 "Damasus Road" experience: I was saved and called at the same time (as I discovered later). How did I discern my Call? Because my passion and the focus of my life shifted to the Kingdom of God. I kept praying as a teenager for direction but later realized the direction I sought had already been given to me. Sometimes people wait and receive the Call. Others, like me, later realize the Call was already on my life. God uses both methods.

One of the ways I confirmed my Call was that sermons, Bible readings, and personal challenges always felt weightier to my soul than as a mere devotional. I heard Paul AI once say: "The Ox was made to pull the plow. The horse was made to pull the wagon. The preacher was made to preach the gospel!" I liken my Call to the encounter Peter had with Jesus in Luke 5, when Peter answered the Call to follow Jesus:

"He (Jesus) got into one of the boats, the one belonging to Simon, and asked him to put out a little from shore." — Luke 5:3 NIV

There was a day at age fourteen that Jesus "got into my boat." From that day on I've lived by this spiritual motto:

1. WHATEVER GOD SAYS, DO IT!

2. WHEREVER GOD LEADS, GO!

3. WHATEVER GOD ASKS, GIVE IT!

Let me leave you with this: The word "Call" has the word "All" embedded in it! GO!

I love to hear stories about the call of God!

I love reading stories from the Bible of great MEN & WOMEN that God called with a specific task!

For example: MOSES ... *freeing the EGYPTIAN SLAVES* ... PARTING THE RED SEA ... *WRITING THE TEN COMMANDMENTS!*

What about DAVID? The KING! The PSALMIST ... We focus on that and immediately feel disqualified, but let's not forget that he started out TENDING SHEEP!

Let me tell you a bit about me that you may not know. In 1984, I moved to Houston and worked at First City Bank for three-and-a-half years! I volunteered as the church youth leader and WORSHIP LEADER. I also took on the responsibility as the KID'S PASTOR. I was at the bottom and was PAID TO CLEAN THE CHURCH until God allowed me to give it up.

One of my favorite Bible Characters is the APOSTLE PAUL ... a church planter, a missionary, and apostle – and who happened to write much of the New Testament!

There's so many more we could explore if we had time, stories of GIDEON, JONAH, and each of the

TWELVE DISCIPLES!

But for the space I have available here, let's focus on
JEREMIAH'S CALL ...

Consider with me three things: THE MYSTERY, THE MAGNITUDE and the MANDATE OF HIS CALL!

Jeremiah 1 introduces us to this great man! He's a PK (preacher's kid). Any PKs out there? He's an ORDINARY YOUNG MAN! He's *cruising through life – minding his own business!*

THEN he has an encounter with God that ***CHANGES HIS WORLD!*** Imagine an ENCOUNTER WITH GOD that literally **changes the TRAJECTORY of YOUR LIFE!**

Jeremiah wakes up one ordinary day to the sound of God speaking with a resounding voice:

> ***"The Word of the Lord came to me saying,***
> ***before I formed you in the womb, I knew you;***
> ***and before you were born, I set you apart."***
> Jeremiah 1:4

I don't know about you, but **that would definitely have gotten my attention!!!**

This wasn't something Jeremiah had SIGNED UP FOR! He hadn't stopped by the REGISTRATION TABLE IN THE CHURCH FOYER and added his name to THE LIST OF "SET APART" CHRISTIANS!

Jeremiah must have thought, *"WHAT DID I REGISTER FOR?"*

If you think about it, the CALL OF GOD is pretty MYSTERIOUS! It's extremely **EXCITING! ADVENTUROUS!**

"The Word of the Lord came to me, saying …"

Which brings us to the MAGNITUDE OF THE CALL!

GOD DOESN'T CALL GREAT PEOPLE TO DO SMALL THINGS! HE CALLS SMALL (seemingly insignificant) PEOPLE TO DO GREAT THINGS!

"… I appointed you a prophet to the nations."

(v. 5)

If I were Jeremiah, I would've been asking … YOU WANT ME TO DO WHAT?

Imagine his task or assignment … In the natural it was an IMPOSSIBLE TASK or MISSION! **He was called to bring the people of Judah back to God at a time when they were on the brink of NATIONAL and SPIRITUAL CATASTROPHE!!!** HE WAS CALLED to be "A PROPHET TO THE NATIONS!"

I mentioned a few moments ago … the MAGNITUDE OF THE CALL … because …

- IT'S GOD WHO DOES THE CALLING!
- People's eternal destiny hangs in the balance awaiting your response!
- The future of GOD'S CHURCH is at STAKE!

I love Jeremiah's response …

"I don't know how to speak; I'm just a child!"

(v. 6)

FUNNY HOW we want to be all GROWN UP until we don't! THE MAGNITUDE OF THE CALL will always give birth to EXCUSES!

You know I'm telling the truth!!!

- I don't know how or where to start.
- I don't think I really understand.
- I couldn't find the right tools or talents.
- I have previous plans.

We've got the MARKET ON EXCUSES!

- I'm too busy!
- I'll defer to someone more qualified!
- Isn't that the youth pastor's job?
- I'm too young! Or too old!

Because of the MAGNITUDE OF THE CALL, excuses seem to come NATURALLY! Still, God says: **I CREATED YOU! I KNOW YOU**, duh? And, I'M CALLING YOU!

Let me ask a question to EVERYONE READING THIS who is currently in MINISTRY: Are you fulfilling your current ministry assignment with an awareness that you are there to impact people for eternity?

Let's look at the MANDATE OF THE CALL!

"YOU MUST go to everyone I SEND YOU TO
and say whatever I command you." (v. 7)

Does anything specific jump out to you? *YOU*
MUST!

God's call changes EVERYTHING! Listen, every
person ever called of God can relate to this! HIS CALL
CHANGES EVERYTHING!

Let me share this moving story of how a *CALL ON*
YOUR LIFE can change everything.

In 2009, a flight attendant for U.S. Airways was
aboard an aircraft that had to ditch in the Hudson River.
Flight attendant Doreen Welsh began attending to the
welfare of her passengers as soon as the aircraft hit the
water. She was so engrossed in HER CALLING TO
SERVE that only after she fought the currents in the river
to get everyone to safety did she notice a serious cut on
her leg that would surely have incapacitated a less
dedicated person! Five people were injured, but thanks to
Doreen and her fellow flight attendants, NO ONE LOST
THEIR LIFE!!

God calls ORDINARY PEOPLE to *do what they'd*

never imagine doing! He WANTS YOU to go WHERE YOU'D never dream of GOING ON YOUR OWN!

MINISTRY IS NOT ABOUT A POSITION OR THE SIZE OF YOUR CHURCH, IT'S ABOUT THE CALL, THE MANDATE!

GOD SPOKE TO JEREMIAH: *Don't let anything keep you from your assignment!*

"DO NOT BE AFRAID!"

FEAR WILL BE YOUR GREATEST OBSTACLE in responding to the CALL! The CALL OF GOD will require steps of FAITH!

Often it won't make SENSE!

Most of the time it's not CONVENIENT!

Don't be AFRAID OF PEOPLE!

Fear of others will immobilize you in ministry! We aren't following PEOPLE! We are following God! INSE-CURITY will imprison you!

I challenge you to **FULFILL GOD'S CALL WITH CONFIDENCE that it's God who called you** and that He is with you every step of the way!

Jeremiah understood this! *Because* ...

- THE **MYSTERY** OF THE CALL should *inspire a sense of AWE* that GOD CALLED US!
- The **MAGNITUDE** OF THE CALL should *create in us a HEART OF HUMILITY and TOTAL DEPENDENCY* ON GOD!
- The **MANDATE** OF THE CALL should cause us to be willing to LAY DOWN OUR LIVES!

I want to warn you that IT WON'T ALWAYS BE GLAMOROUS! EVERYONE IN MINISTRY HAS THREATENED TO QUIT AT LEAST ONCE!

In the 20th chapter of Jeremiah, things aren't going exactly as Jeremiah had envisioned. He was:

- ARRESTED
- BEATEN
- PUT IN STOCKS
- FINALLY RELEASED!

Verse 7 gives us Jeremiah's reaction, the raw version that his congregation never saw. Here is REALITY ...

Jeremiah said, ***"Oh Lord, you misled me, and I allowed it! I am mocked and made fun of EVERY DAY! Laughed at! This job has brought me INSULT and***

REPROACH!"

Even so, a few verses down, Jeremiah goes on to say: ***"GOD, YOUR WORD IS LIKE A FIRE THAT BURNS IN MY HEART and IN MY BONES!"***

The MANDATE will cause you to be willing to take ABUSE or even LAY DOWN YOUR LIFE!

In 2013, Pastor Saeed Abedini was imprisoned in Iran and sentenced for eight years all because of his FAITH!

On March 17, his son, Jacob, was to celebrate his seventh birthday, so he created

Pastor Saeed Abedini

a hand-made invitation for his father.

I'll read Pastor Saeed's response.

To my beloved son, Jacob:

I received the beautiful birthday invitation and know how much you want me to be there for your celebration. Please know that I love you very much.

I long to be there for your birthday, but my chains are keeping me from you!

I want you to know that although I am not able to and you will feel my absence, there is ONE who is always there with you. He can meet your needs under any condition.

I won't be there on your birthday and that breaks my heart as your father. But, I know ONE who is always there and cares for you more than anyone could. He is there with you and his name is – "I AM WHO I AM!"

"I AM WHO I AM" means that God is with you in every situation. This is the name Jehovah used to IDENTIFY HIMSELF when meeting Moses at the BURNING BUSH.

The people Moses was called to lead were CRYING OUT and you have every reason as well!

But, let me assure you I AM WHO I AM is there with you, son! Receive Him – accept Him!

Happy birthday, Jacob, you're a BIG BOY and A HERO to me! Thank you for standing strong with me in this battle for the GLORY OF

OUR LORD and SAVIOR JESUS CHRIST!
Signed – YOUR PROUD DAD!

I invite you to RENEW YOUR CALL! If you're new to CALLED CAMP, maybe you need to CONFIRM YOUR CALL!

For everyone reading this, our experiences vary. You may be here, and this is your first time at CALLED CAMP. Others have ATTENDED FOR THE THREE YEARS since we began.

Still, GOD IS REVEALING YOUR SPECIFIC STORY! I AM WHO I AM continues to reveal His plan for YOUR LIFE.

I want you to take a sheet of paper and a pen and put YOUR STORY ON PAPER.

THE MYSTERY ...

THE MAGNITUDE ...

THE MANDATE ...

Say to the Lord, "I GIVE MYSELF AWAY, SO YOU CAN USE ME!"

Perhaps your story will one day be shared at a CALLED CAMP ... to encourage and inspire others who are in pursuit of the CALLING OF GOD.

I can't wait to see your story DEVELOP ... RIGHT NOW IT MAY SEEM SO SIMPLE ... SO BORING ... BUT God is using you ...

Don't discredit humble beginnings ... GOD IS WRITING YOUR STORY!

In the following pages, I would like to share a collection of stories from the attendees at CALLED CAMP 2025. Some of these have been edited for clarity or readability, but each retains the TENDER AND HEARTFELT TRUTH of the Call that God has put on each of these young hearts. For privacy, only initials are used for names, with anonymous submissions marked as An.

God still moves on the youth of today, and they ARE THE CHURCH OF THE FUTURE. Young people, I can hardly wait to see where God leads you tomorrow, the day after, and ALL THE DAYS OF YOUR LIFE!

Your story is now in God's hands! How exciting is that?!?

God show me what you want from me.
I look my age but inside I'm still young.
I feel like the young girl still searching
for more. I am a single parent confused
of what you want from me. Told that I'm
not enough but you tell me I'm more than
enough. Scared to direct my children some
where I call unknown. How can I lead
if I still feel like I need to be led?
God direct me. Show me the path. Use me
to help others who are lost. Calm my fears
and give me peace. More of you and less
of me. That when the time comes I know
I did not do this on my own. God take
my vision off of me and onto you. Direct
me Lord. Help me to know its not too late

GOD HAS CALLED ME!

God's Calling as Shared by Attendees at
CALLED CAMP/2025

MY STORY: I gave my life to Christ in 2021 at youth camp and have forever been changed. I have always been in love with medicine and the medical field. God has put me on a path to grow my knowledge. When I graduate high school, I will have three certifications, a diploma, and an associate degree. God has called me into the ministry to spread the Gospel and the love of Jesus Christ to those who don't know it, those out of reach, and those in need of His saving. But God hasn't forgotten my call into medicine. Once I graduate high school, I will attend MS State, continue to grow my faith, and bring people into this life while also studying to become a doctor. God has called me to be a medical missionary, to be a doctor at home, but also to travel to places in need or out of reach of medical help. I will spread the Gospel and use the talent and passion God has given me to help those in need while making room to help others instead of myself. I thank God for what He has done in my life, and I can't wait to see what He does in the future through me, building His kingdom and making heaven crowded. ~AC

I FEEL MY calling is to be a youth pastor. I have always had a fear of praying for random people, but it was at church camp when God used me to answer a random kid's prayer who I'd never talked to. God showed me that I'd be a youth pastor and perhaps someday a lead pastor. For now, I just thank Him for all the blessings He's put into my life. 1 Peter 1:13-16 ~SV

WHAT DOES MY future look like? SAGU/Nelson University with a ministry degree, perhaps participation in track & field? I feel God saying, "I have put the desire and love for track in your heart for a reason, and I the

Lord your God will have my way and open up doors. I, Son, will hear you so you can pursue this dream of yours. But, stay close to me, draw near to me, train hard, be disciplined, and I will make this desire of yours, this passion, come true. Even when it looks impossible, am I not the miracle worker? I will make the way for you to be at SAGU/Nelson University in this next season of college. My ways are above and beyond anything and everything. I will make clear the pathway I have for you. I have already ordained your steps, my son. Just take my hand as I lead you. I am your Father!" ~NG

I AM BEING used in youth. God is teaching me to be used in Spanish and building up a church. ~AF

WELL, RIGHT NOW I'm serving in kid's ministries, but I want to spread the Word in my school. This is because I see that some people are lost, and I want them to find their path with the Lord, including my friends. ~SP

I WANT TO be a part of a youth ministry, perhaps as a youth leader, because I feel that God is calling me. I just want to serve my youth pastors for everything they have done to grow me as a person. I was a very shy, depressed kid, and when I first visited the youth group at Faith Church, everything changed. My personality changed! I thank my mom for being there for me throughout this journey. The Lord answered prayers, as my mom and my aunt were the ones who stood with me and helped me. They helped me become a better person. I want to tell my story to other teenagers who are dealing with the same issues I dealt with. They need to know how good God has been to me and that Jesus literally changed my life. ~GL

GOD, THANK YOU for letting me serve in children's church and for allowing me the opportunity to preach in my youth group. Thank You, God, for putting my leaders, E. and his wife, in my life when I needed them! ~TT

LAST YEAR I had a vision at a summer camp where I was called into youth ministry. The reason I registered for Called Camp was to explore that call. I've started by making myself available to pray with people, and it feels good. I want to be obedient, saying YES to God and the calling, or go through any open door God gives me. I'm grateful for good friends and my supportive family who are on this path with me, encouraging and supporting me. ~LB

FATHER, I THANK You for my life, my friends and family, and for all the people You've placed in my life. I come to the altar on my knees asking You to complete Your will in my life. I love serving kids and youth, but I have a strong connection in worship, and I'm not sure I know what You want from me. All I want is for my call to be what you want whether it's singing for kids or being a pastor. I am scared, but with You I can do anything. Your servant is waiting for You to tell me what I must do to serve the One and Only! ~EZ

GOD HAS SHOWN me that I will preach and lead people in worship. My prayer is that I will lead many to Jesus. He has shown me the way, and I will serve Him all the days of my life. I was saved from addiction, suicide and self-harm. He is truly my Redeemer. ~KM

MY STORY AND calling are to lead people to Christ, because in the moments I am alone, crying out to God, He reminds me that He and others have been there for me. I need to be like Jesus and willing to give myself for others no matter the cost, while always chasing a better, deeper relationship with God, and being willing to serve wherever He leads. I want Him to make me bold in my witness and to be happy with nothing but Jesus. ~GJ

My story:
- Grew up in a Christian home - VERY christian ☺
- Had everything I could ask for - fam, friends, church
- Relied heavily on my friends & material things
- Moved to Houston - left everything → broke my heart
- Felt like I had NOBODY, no friends, no church, nothing
- Then I realized my identity isn't found by my friends
- God put people in my life ♡
- Even when I had nobody, I still had God & that was everything I could ever ask for & all I needed.
- Thank you Jesus for being my best friend & for all the people you put in my life ♡
- I want to minister to kids - the children of this generation. I want to leave my comfort zone. But it doesn't matter what I want. It's what God wants. So God, please use me & show me. Thank you.

—CALLED CAMP/2025——— CT

I WILL BE A WITNESS!

God's Calling as Shared by Attendees at
CALLED CAMP/2025

I WAS BAPTIZED at my church when I was seven years old. When I went under the water, I remember coming up and saying, "Amen." Tears were flowing down my face, and my hands were reaching high into the air in praise to God. I didn't know at that age what "JEHOVAH" meant but remember speaking it repeatedly. Falling on my knees, I started singing songs that were new to me. I want to be used of God! ~CY

I HAVE BEEN a Christian since I was five years old, and people have always said to me that one day I would become a pastor. One day I went to church, and the children were having a mini children's night. One of the leaders from the children's ministry asked me to help. He said they'd also be serving food, so of course I agreed. The next day I got a call from my Tia who said they were having a meeting with all the helpers, so I went. They told us they wanted all who had helped to become part of the children's ministries on Sundays. So, for six years now I have been part of the children's ministries but hope one day in the future to become a pastor. It's all in God's will. ~SQ

I THINK AND believe God has called me to pastor. I'm going to college for it, but I don't think it ends there. I feel there is more, but I've been struggling. ~J

GOD, THANK YOU for Your continued patience with me and for all that You've shown me. My story may not have the most exciting beginning, but I do see Your hand guiding me and recognize Your leading. You place people in my life to guide me and to show me what Your love looks like. You've shown me what sacrifice looks like and what discipleship looks like. I felt I didn't deserve a friend like D., but You still placed him in my life. Without even realizing it, I was learning and growing from all that I saw in him. I know realize that it was because he said yes to You and no to a lot of things. I pray and ask that You give me a heart like that, a heart that says no to everything else and yes to You! ~JM

THE LORD HAS given me a passion to talk about the Bible and tell people what the Lord has done for me. I feel called to be a pastor. God has given me a hunger for wisdom and Him. He has given me confidence, and I am available as He guides me. ~SG

FROM THE BEGINNING, I knew I could sing. What I did not know was that it was not only a gift but a calling. No matter what anyone tells me, I know God's voice. I will keep pursuing You, Lord, in whatever or wherever

You are calling me to. This is only the beginning. Lord, thank You for placing me in positions that test me. Thank You for all the people that pushed me to my calling. Lastly, thank You for Your confirmation in where You are telling me I need to be. Lord, continue speaking to me no matter how far I get from You. My story continues ...
~ES

I DIDN'T KNOW what my call was when I first got here, but now I believe God is calling me to be part of the worship team. Now that I say this, I remember being part of the worship team when I was younger. I used to sing with my sister and our close friend, the pastor's granddaughter. I think God is calling me to be a part of the band now, since I am part of my school's band. I could use my experience in that to get better and more confident. ~MP

LORD, I AM so thankful for the life You have given me. One thing I am most thankful for is the parents You have put in my life. If I wasn't raised in church, I wouldn't see myself joining one on my own or trying it out. I do not feel I am at Called Camp for reasons like others. I feel distanced. I pray and often still feel this way. When I read the Bible, I feel lost and don't know what to do. I'm open to You. I feel I am here to learn how to keep a steady relationship with You. I resubmit and commit my life to You and keeping that commitment. ~JH

GOD, THANK YOU for beginning this story/testimony for me to share with others. Thank You so much for the people You have surrounded me with: parents, sisters, friends, etc… These people, with Your influence, have helped me to see You, although they may not even know it. God, I also want to say thanks for the story that is to come in my life. Thanks for preparing me to do great things in Your name. I am a warrior, and I pray that everything I do will be in love, and that I will constantly seek Your kingdom and Your face. J. in India asked me to give away a pair of new shoes I recently received. I've been given several dreams about this and now know that

God was preparing my heart for His service. His perfect timing all started before I recognized that He was moving or using me or even speaking to me. So, God, thank You for taking me on this journey to be Your servant. I pray for greater love, humility, and understanding that only You can give. I also pray for sensitivity to You. I pray that everything You do will not leave me, and I pray that I will act as if it were my last opportunity. Use me for Your glory! ~AT

LORD, I DON'T know how or why You would ever call a girl like me, but I know You took a broken little girl like me and helped me know through faith that I am not alone. God, You were my friend when others rejected this awkward girl with autism. You were there for me! I may not get how You will continue to write my story, but You will. I love You and pray You'll make me bold like the women in the Bible. Use me, Lord! ~NL

Just like to thank you for the path you've given me. Youth ministry is what you've spoken to me, so I will continue to have faith in it. I know you'll open the doors for College into GLC. You've already given me Amity there like I've prayed for. I know ya'll continue to set the path through trusting you Lord. You've had people speak over my life + you've always had someone to help me when I've started doubting. Thank you.

Thank you for the people you've brought to me, to help me, change me, impact me, even when I didn't except it, or apply it. Thank you for the opportunities i've been blessed with. I trust you, I won't doubt you, because I know you are good and have done great things in my life. Even the tough times. You pulled me through, and used those struggles to shape me. I've been blessed with the experience to feel your touch, in hard. The feeling of you saving me from my sin and shame, pulling me into your arms, From now on forward, i don't know my call, but I know my God and all I can do is trust him, seek him, and allow him to use me.

MAKE ME STRONG FOR YOU!

God's Calling as Shared by Attendees at
CALLED CAMP/2025

I DIDN'T KNOW what to write, so I just prayed. I was feeling overwhelmed with all the calling, but God gave me the message that I can do all things with Him. Just be obedient, and all of the crazy, impossible plans I have will be fulfilled. I am not perfect, and I've made so many mistakes. But, His grace covers me, and His plan will prevail. I surrender and will do it God's way! Not mine! I will make room – I am called, and I am ready! ~NP

LORD, YOU HAVE given me so much and, Lord, I thank You for it! I've seen You work in my life. You have allowed me to work on stages and preach, and I thank You, Lord. Thank You for the sensitivity you've given me to Your presence. I now ask You, Lord, to use all the gifts You have given me to reach others for You. You've done it in the life of my grandpa and my dad, so please continue with me! Lord, direct me as You reveal and light my path. Lord, help me to desire You and keep near You. Humble me if needed and grow me in new areas in my faith and ministry. Lord, help me in my unbelief when I am doubting and confused about what my calling is. Thank You, Lord, for everything, and if it's Your will, let it be. ~AM

I STARTED TO follow God and accept Him completely when I was fourteen. I was brought up in church and always had a connection with Him, yet I went through things that made me distance myself from Him. A person that really helped open my eyes and pushed me to God was my cousin. She showed how God really is and how God helped her. I started going to youth service where I met my youth pastors who believed in me and provided guidance. They gave me opportunities to get closer to God. My parents were supportive but had their own struggles, yet still they pushed me toward church and God. I've found that God is always there, and during times I've felt all alone or left behind, He was there watching over me and caring for me. He's always provided for my every need. ~MD

THE MYSTERY of the Call: How do I reach people on a larger scale? YouTube, Instagram and Social Media! *The Magnitude of the Call:* My musical callings can inspire someone with the same calling. Just as I admire and watch musicians, someone could do the same to me. *The Mandate of the Call:* If I don't respond to my call, then I might not be used to inspire others who could be. I must follow God to reach people in music and all areas. Father, forgive me of my sins and the times I ran away from You. This weekend, I come back to You. I rededicate my life to You, Lord, in Jesus' name. Amen. Father God, why do I feel connected to Moses? What is it about his story that resonates with me? God, open my eyes and mind and to hear what You're telling me, whether through Moses or in my life. Help me remain confident in my faith and stay strong in You. I love You, Lord. The Great I Am! Make me a strong lion for You, Lord. ~JA

WHAT IS GOD calling me to do? He is calling me to be a leader in a middle school girls' group. He is calling me to be a camp leader and somewhere on the mission field. I feel that I am to lead youth and help the broken to be a vessel for Him. I want to make people feel welcome and understood and to be bold in bringing people to Jesus. I want to do everything to the glory of God. What God has already done in my life amazes me. He has allowed me to serve with the 4-to-6-year-olds, teach K-6, and be a light on sports teams. He saved me for a reason! ~SM

I GOT MY CALLING around three-and-a-half years ago. I believe I am called to be a lead pastor. For a while I didn't know where to start, but I felt led into tech ministries. A lot has changed since I got my calling, several ups and downs. Some were worse than others. But I've found myself lost, struggling with worldly desires and temptations with no clue where to look for help or a next step. I came here today hoping to find guidance and a place to turn to. ~KH

LORD, THANK YOU for everyone that has worked at youth camp. Thank You for my friends and my mother. Ever since You came back into my life, everything is better. I preach Your Word sometimes without even thinking about it. I forgive my father and those who have forsaken me. Today, I want to experience everything I can have. One day I pray that I will be able to explain how You've helped me. I want You to be the center of everything I do. You worked in my disorder and gave me people to talk to. You gave me peace in chaos. When I strayed from You, You brought me back home. ~IC

I HONESTLY don't know what is to happen with my life. I've been through some things. I've done some things. I know I'm not worthy of Him or His love. Yet I still strive for His warmth and love. I recently found out that due to medical conditions, I'm not able to do my dream job. I suppose God has other plans. I'm lost. I have no idea in which direction my life is going. I hope to follow God's will but at the same time, I want to know why this has happened to me. Why me, Lord? I've tried to stay loyal. I've failed. What is going to happen to me? ~MM

I FEEL THE Lord has called me into serving through opportunities I'm currently involved in, like theater. I am called to preach, speak and share with my peers. God, I will follow wherever You're leading me, one step at a time. I don't know exactly where my calling is leading, but I'll trust You every single day. As I follow, I know He will guide me like He always has. ~N

What is God doing in my life
I think that God uses me when I felt called to help out making my highschool Jesus club.

My story is a little boring but I know I was called to this came to grow closer to him because I know he saw me drifting away. I thank God for this like he gave me and the people he put in 4 like Julia and my grandma. The most God fearing people I have ever met and they help me in so many ways without realising. I thank God for putting me through everything that has happened to me because it made me who I am today and bettered me as a person. Following the Lord has saved my life and I believe my calling one day will be in youth ministry and to help kids and teens grow their faith more and more everyday. Even when I helped clean up inside the church that was a way God used me as a sort of vessel.

I pray over my family and friends, that you help them and bless them through everything they go through and that you heal my heart of temptation and you wash/clean me because I want to surrender my all to you, and I want to be pure in your holy name, thank you Jesus for the opportunity to come to called camp and for this wonderful life in your holy name I pray, Amen.

YOU ARE MY OPEN DOOR!

God's Calling as Shared by Attendees at
CALLED CAMP/2025

THANK YOU FOR opening many doors. Thank You for giving me breath in my lungs. Thank You for L., M., and C. I've been going through something that I need to surrender. I'm scared, and I don't know why. I don't want to give up but feel that I'm being held down by the enemy. This struggle has been going on for a while, and I know I need to give it up, but there is something holding me back and I know why. Tonight, January 2, 2025, I'm giving You my whole heart. This is a part of my story. and it's time for God to get the pen and start writing, not me. It's time for a chapter and for my chains to be broken. Thank You, Jesus. In July 2022, Jesus became real to me at my youth camp. I was filled with the Holy Spirit, and I read my Bible more and more. I felt so close to Him. Then I started hanging around the wrong crowd and started going down a bad path. I am restoring my relationship with God, and HE IS MOVING! ~PW

DEAR LORD, I thank You for choosing me as one of Your servants. I am surprised but in a good way. There's a fire in me for tech/media ministry and to preach, so help me do it without fear. I thank You for pastors like PZ and M. and the other leaders—G., D. and T.—to guide me. I thank You for my church friends that are with me when I need someone. I thank you for S. and pray that she's aligned with Your plan and not mine. I love You, trust You, and with all my might want You! ~DC

SOMETIMES I FEEL that God isn't watching over me. In the past year one of my family members died. I remember praying and expressing my love for God but asking that my family member doesn't die. My grandpa was on dialysis and on the edge of dying, but when death came for him, he didn't die but lived for year. It gave me a chance to let him know how much I love him and say my goodbyes. All I can imagine is how grandpa must have felt when he received his ultimate healing. God's plan has allowed many miracles in my family, and I like to say His plans don't fail. I feel called to spread the Word and follow it. I want to be an example of Jesus to my grandma before she dies and walks through the gates of Heaven to be with Jesus. ~ET

THANK YOU, LORD, for the opportunities You've given me! Lord, I ask You to use me whatever my calling is. I pray You will use me to show other people Your love in the same way someone showed me. God, I want You to use me like the people You've placed in my life. You gave them to me when You couldn't physically reach me, and I am forever grateful for that. I want to show the most broken people how much You love them and that they are here for a reason. God, I'm not sure what that means, but if that is for me to become a youth pastor, God, use me to show young people that they aren't alone and to show them that there is a God who loves them and will meet their needs. You will never leave them alone. God, I don't know what Your calling is for me and what my life will look like, but like Pastor Tim said, this isn't scary. God, You've brought me this far, and I need You to lead me on the path and show me the plan. Three years ago, I wanted to leave church and even doubted Your existence at times. But, if You've brought me this far, I can only imagine where You will take me. Thank You for all the blessings in my life, and I hope I can fulfill whatever it is that You have called me to do. ~M

MY TESTIMONY is one of the most important things in my life. It makes me thankful for where I am today. I have nobody else to thank for all the blessings I've got. I think my story started when I was eight years old. In 2014 my father passed away due to a heart attack. I didn't know God at that time, but I remember thinking, "WHY IS THIS HAPPENING?" My dad's death really impacted me in so many ways. It has helped show me what God can do for me. The day I was saved is a blur, and I don't remember much except the joy I received. I am grateful that God brought me to Crossroads Fellowship. I am what I am today because of the lessons I've learned and the timing of God to work things out in my life. I want to continue to learn to be more like Him. ~AA

I FEEL THAT I am being called to be a musician. I want to help people with my music and expand the Kingdom of God by leading people to Christ. ~TP

I'VE GROWN UP in church. I've always known and loved God, but around the age of twelve or thirteen, I lost my true identity. I was lost and confused. I went to camp at age fifteen and thought I was radically changed, but I wasn't. I've always battled fear and anxiety, but by seeking first the kingdom of God, I found love and passion for the Lord through worship, missions and children's ministries. So, how can I be worried about tomorrow when I know the plans God has for me are holy? I am convinced that God has a mighty plan! I want everyone to know Jesus, and it's hard for me to know they won't. I'm going to try to do my part. I'm fearfully and wonderfully made. Though I've been through trials and hardships, I know God is calling me through my brokenness. One thing is certain, I am called, and I thank You, Jesus! ~AM

MY STORY IS still being worked on. I feel like it is set for me to help the world and people in poverty from around the world that don't have food to eat. It is important for me to help them with their problems but also in spreading the Word so they might find their way with the Lord. I know my story has been rough, all the things I've done, not very Christian-like, but I'm changing. I'm trying. It's been a slow process, but I know this process takes time. ~An.

Lord I believe you've called me father
and I thank you for what you have used
me for already Lord, I thank you for placing
me at my home church father. I'm sorry
if I have ever taken where I am today
for granted. Lord I'm trusting in and the
plan that you have for me Lord I know
that your timings right father, Lord I'm
sorry for seeing muself less than
others because I think I'm not up to
the standard to be used by you Lord.
Lord take all the time that you need to
revele yourself to me, I want to wait
for you so i'll be here Lord with an
opean heart ready to say yes to whatever
and where ever your calling me to. Lord
teach me how to be patient in this
waiting secene you have me in father.
give me eyes and ears to see and hear
you father I come to you with a heart
that is willing to listen. Lord let me
be content on all of the things I have
and the things I'm doing now. Lord Let
me not grow werry on where you have
me father Let me do ever thing with
Love and happiness even if i'm doing
the same things for the next couple of
years Lord. I thank you for all you've
already done in my life Lord and
everyday I will choose to live for you
I thank you father and love you, Amen.

My Story Is Worth Telling!

God's Calling as Shared by Attendees at
CALLED CAMP/2025

AS A SEVEN-YEAR-OLD boy, I accepted Jesus as my savior, and it was the first decision I truly felt I made. Later that year, I felt God put a calling on my life and a burden on my heart. If I'm being honest, I often feel like that seven-year-old boy who fell in love with his savior. I've grown healthier as a person through Jesus. I've grown more and more passionate for Him, His coming back, and His will. I know He has a plan for my life. I feel that I want Him more than anything, but at times my feet feel stuck. Although I said yes, I've not done anything lately to grow in that relationship. But, in Jesus' name, that all changes today. Holy Spirit, I need Your baptism and power to be what You've called me to be. ~JG

GROWING UP I'VE always thought my story was not worth telling. I thought that because I was born into a Christian home with godly parents that I had an easy life. Still, I began to drift away from God, and if I'm being honest, I never really had my own relationship with God. I've done things I knew I shouldn't do but compared myself to others who didn't even go to church. Somehow, I felt superior and justified. This became an excuse for other things in my life. My parents saw the struggle and began looking for a church for us to attend where I'd be challenged. I remember the first sermon the pastor spoke, and for the first time I genuinely felt God's presence. It was there I realized how God really loves me. ~SP

MY HEART HURTS for those who hurt and don't know You. I am willing to lay down my time, personal feelings, and wants to help others. When I first saw Called Camp fliers for 2023, I was intrigued to go. I never wanted to be a missionary. My plans were always to have a huge house, a big family, and lots of money. Instead, in Called Camp, I found that God wanted my "yes." I couldn't stand and fell to my knees saying, "Here I am, God. I'll go wherever You call me. I'll go, please send me." Since then, I've faced trials and achieved a lot of growth. I've gone to El Salvador and worked with kid's camps there. I accept and say yes to my call, and whether it is near or far, I'll go. I say YES all over again! ~M

I THANK GOD that I have a story to tell. All the obstacles that I've faced have brought me closer to God. It all started my sophomore year as I was being bullied, and a friend invited me to Church of Hope. Even though I grew up in church, I hadn't made my own relationship with Him yet. After that first visit, I made new friends who showed me compassion and friendship. Even though the bullying continued my junior year, God gave me grace and compassion for that person. I've learned that I can trust God to lead me, because He knows the steps I take. I've loved serving my church and the homeless in our area. I don't know God's exact calling on my life, but I do know that He has put a love for helping others in my heart. I pray for continued direction and clarification. I love You, God, and thank You for all I've experienced in my life, because it's made me the person I am today. You've taught me through these things to show kindness, grace, and compassion while sharing Your Word. I pray that others who need help will find You as I have. Thank you, God, for everything You've done in my story, past, present, and future. I love You. And, while I am still uncertain on my path, I know You will guide me. I seek You and know You have a great future ahead for me. ~A

THANK YOU FOR the blessing that You gave me of strength to continue. I felt that I was to become a nurse but might have messed up. I don't know where You want me, but all I know is that I want to serve You no matter what. You were there for me when I was lost, and I'm glad You didn't give up on me. Now, I want to move in sync with You, and I want Your will accomplished in my life. Please continue building me, and I ask You to take me where I need to go. Don't let me be a failure. Give me Your victory, because You know the plan. ~M

THANK YOU, LORD, for dying for me and the people out there who still need You. Your love illuminates so brightly with the type of love that feels like a best friend, mom, father, or sibling. Your love turns hurt into happiness. Thank You for always being by my side and guiding me through my calling. I want to be able to share Your love and be the light in the world (Matt. 5:16). I want to thank You for being there for me when I've felt alone and for helping me realize that if I want to meet people and share Your love, I have to open myself to Your plan. Doing Your work isn't easy. I will keep walking in Your ways and get a better understanding of Your Word. I love you, Lord, and am thankful that You're my best friend. ~AM

MY STORY IS just getting to the good part. Since I can remember, I've been in church. I've always loved music and listening to different kinds. Before I was born, my mom was taken in by my god-grandparents. They are the family God gave me since my birth. I've loved drums and started to play at church at the age of three. I've been playing drums ever since. I've always felt a call to do more. I remember following my grandpa around with a microphone (not turned on) and mimicking him preaching. I know I am called, so show me, use me and change me, Lord. Your way is better. I trust Your Word in Isaiah 54:17: "No weapon formed against me shall prosper." ~DA

I THANK GOD for all the mission trips I've made with my mom and dad. Thank You for all the ideas I have been having of being an inventor. And, thank You for allowing me to fly a plane. I remember a specific trip to Uraguay, which was life-giving, seeing all the children and adults happy. Use me, Lord! ~M

God's calling on my life started young: to worship Him. Leading songs and dances in children's ministry. I was on fire to worship Him. When I left kid's ministry I went into youth, where I learned more about worship, encouraged by my leaders like Cheyann and Kris and Julie and Frank to continue to dance and sing onto the Lord, no matter how I sounded or looked. No fear, just me and my Jesus. My heart of worship grew there. I audition for youth worship when I was 16. I grew my voice within the team for years, doubt and moments of solitude came but when I was ready to step off, God always pulled me back up. I continued to serve in worship anyway I could and when I had very little and thanked God; He gave me more. He entrusted me with leading worship for a ministry. YA Worship. I had to overcome struggle like Pride, impatience, anger, and bitterness and learned to be a graceful leader, a patient, kind, understanding one. I had to surrender fully to God and dive into the fire so he could refine me; purify me. Trials weren't easy but I have a calling to fufill and leaders/pastors who trusted me to fufill it. I thank God for pulling me back to worship, for never giving up on me, never losing hope - no matter how many times I stumble. Thank you Lord for calling me! Putting me into your worship, the privillege to usher in your presence. I know I dont deserve it, yet you still trust me to share your glory. The best is yet to come! Amen.

I ACCEPT MY CALLING!

God's Calling as Shared by Attendees at
CALLED CAMP/2025

GOD, I WANT to thank you for my family, friends, and opportunities You've given me! I feel that You are pushing me towards ministry and that You want to change people's lives through me. You've started by giving me the opportunity to help in kid's ministries. Even though I rejected You, You took me in and healed me and put me back together. I wish to help others in the way that I've been helped. I accept my calling! ~JO

LORD, I THANK You for the opportunities I've been given. Thank You for the strength, wisdom, courage, and fortitude to follow You. Lord, I know there is still more to my story, and I have a purpose from You. Use me, Lord, to reach people, to help and love those in need. Use all my imperfections and everything that I am as a part of my calling. I wholeheartedly surrender and accept whatever you have for me. I am your vessel to show the world the real you. ~AF

LORD, I AM called to pastoral ministry. I don't know what all my calling entails, but I trust You. Lord, I surrender my desire to be used by You. Lead me wherever You want me to go. ~A

I WAS TWELVE when I first started attending church. My pastor, A. C., and I became close. One day I told him about a funny sermon idea … "I'm not hatin', I'm just state'n." He responded with, "Let me know when it's written, and you can preach it." I thought he was joking, but two months later he texted me asking how the sermon was going. I was given the assignment to preach it in youth service that next Wednesday night. I was scared, but because of his faith in me, I couldn't let him down. That next week I preached and later preached it on Sunday. (I've now preached four sermons.) The next week, Pastor A. told me about fine arts, a place where youth could use their talents, so he signed me up. Now, through Pastor A., I am at Called Camp where students can learn more about their own calling, and I love it. ~BH

I GREW UP in a Baptist church, and when I was five, my parents got divorced. It was not until ten years later that I found out the real reason. The home I grew up in was in bad shape, creating anxiety for me. My clothes, my life, everything was a disappointment and a mess. When I was thirteen, I lost my pawpaw, and it literally crushed me. I am thankful for my best friend who saw me in need and invited me to get right with God. For the first time, I felt loved in the presence of God, a love like never before. I started attending church but through some unfortunate situations left. Later, I met my boyfriend who invited me to church and reintroduced me to the Lord. When I first went to summer camp, I saw kids like me that seemed lost. I realized I am called to be a leader, one who directs them back to God, regardless how broken. ~KP

I NEVER REALLY felt like God was calling me into anything in my life, but now I'm realizing that I might be called into full-time ministry. Or maybe I am called to help people heal their hurting in a godly way instead of turning to the world for healing. I feel the Lord telling me to continue to trust His plans and His path for me. As I learn from my mistakes, I can use that to lead more people to Christ. My pain and sorrow can help people from hurting themselves even more. I want to help people who feel helpless. No matter what. I want to continue to trust what the Lord has in store for me. ~LC

YOU CALLED ME back to Radius! You set me free at Agora! You placed me as a leader for Youth Alive, youth group, and Sunday school. You gave me a new armor of silver and gold. You have allowed me to engage in conversation with you. You call me your prophet and a teacher, and more recently you put me in a pastoral position. Lord, I thank You for making my life exciting. I love You and Your call! Even though I feel inadequate, You're the one who readies me and prepares me. ~JN

I DON'T EXACTLY know my calling yet. I am a greeter and play some instruments. I try to bring my friends to church and influence them using scripture verses from the Bible. I speak in kid's church and am grateful for the opportunity. ~HS

I FEEL LIKE God has called me to kid's ministry as of right now. I have been told by many parents how their kids look up to me and want to become like me. I just feel so thankful to God for allowing me to encourage and guide others, and I feel so thankful to God for allowing me to support the next generation. Even when I feel like I do too many wrong things or feel that I am not fit to lead and guide others, He always comes in at the right time and reassures me that He is not done with me. I feel called to missions where I live, to my home country, or wherever God leads me. I pray that He will reveal His plan. ~DH

GROWING UP AS a preacher's kid, at times my life felt useless and draining. Now I realize it's all part of my story. Being at church all the time kept me from trying to figure out who I wanted to be and was depressing at times. I felt trapped! It was when I started volunteering that I realized it was my opportunity to share God's glory. I realize now just how blessed I am. Now I feel called and am involved in media, photography, kid's church, praise & worship, and am willing to do anything else God needs me to do. ~N

From a very young age I went to church. I've been going to church ever since. But I never really got connected in the church. Until one day we started going to this one church that we all started getting connected in. I was very shy and did not like to anyone at all. But this church changed me. I started growing a deep relationship with the Lord and He led me to get more connected in the church. I started going to the youth group services they had on Wednesdays. As I continued to grow my relationship with the Lord He healed me from anxiety, fear, and shyness. Now that He has opened up my voice, He has called me to help send revival to this generation in our schools, youth, and everyone around me. He has also called me in this season to preach the word in a group our church has for young men, middle school through highschool. And I beleive He is calling me to preach His word to this generation.

FOLLOWING GOD'S PATH!

God's Calling as Shared by Attendees at
CALLED CAMP/2025

I ACCEPTED the Lord in kindergarten, and it was the greatest decision I've made. Although sometimes I think getting saved as a child isn't much of a testimony, I've learned that I have a testimony of trusting God. Even when everything I've known seemed to be in chaos, God was still there. When it seemed that my whole world had walked out the door, I remembered to turn to God. I leaned on the Scriptures that I was taught from a young age. I feel a very heavy calling to kids and youth ministry. My whole childhood I searched and found God accessible even to a young child. Even when I wasn't mature enough to know what to do, I knew to pray. I want to be that person who can walk through life with the next generation, helping other kids that are just like me. God has led me to influence kid's lives and be that role mode. even while I'm still in high school. The best feeling comes from hearing kids' stories, praying with them, and them knowing I am proud of them and will be there for them. ~SG

I HAVE A GOOD community of God-followers. I help with the lighting in the church and feel that it's what I'm made to do. I feel great having Jesus inside of me and being full of the Holy Spirit. This opportunity to attend Called Camp is a great way for me to be strengthened in my relationship with God. ~OG

I AM CURRENTLY thirteen years old and have had some bumps in the road. But I have a good God who sent me great leaders who've helped me in my bad times. Like Pastor J. who has loved me through my highs and lows. My God has always been there for everything in my life.

I currently serve in kid's ministries, tech team, and pre-K, and I love when I get to serve. I want the focus to be on Him and off me. It feels so natural when I stand to serve the kids. It feels like what I am doing has an impact on people, and I love that. ~ES

WHAT ARE YOU called to? Kid's ministry, but it's hard because I don't want to give up what I love. ~ID

GOD USES ME by guiding my words to other people as I tell and/or show them who God is. In other instances, if they are having a tough time, He uses me in prayer to bless them. ~TF

WHEN I WAS seven or eight, I was at Kids' Camp, and that night's service was about how God can use anyone. Several people including me felt a calling that night. Being a teacher and worship leader in kid's ministry was my specific calling. I cried, saying I didn't want to work with kids, but throughout the rest of camp, and in the years since, the calling has grown. ~JH

I HAVE FACED many temptations that I have fallen into, but through it all, God knows my heart. I've never wanted to hurt anybody or do wrong. God is going to take where I have fallen and teach me how to be mature and make decisions that Jesus makes. God is writing a great story for me that I believe will bring Him glory. ~C

I WAS BORN and raised in Tennessee until the age of six when we moved to Houston in April 2016. The next year I was baptized even though I was completely unaware what it meant. Fast forward to the age of eleven, when I started watching adult videos, which led me to do bad things and brought my self-esteem down. This went on until the age of thirteen, when I officially gave my life to Christ. I started helping my kid's pastor on the children's ministry staff and volunteering in the nursery. I am praying about getting baptized again now that I know the full meaning of it, and I feel called to full-time children's ministry. ~AC

MY STORY IS like many others. I've struggled with lust for almost half of my life but have felt that God wants to do something in my life. My youth pastor, C., has helped pave the way for my relationship with Jesus, showing me what it really means to be a true and faithful Christian. It was at youth camp that I first felt a calling to get closer to God and share His gospel. I desire to share with others that Jesus desires a relationship from us, not religion. There is my small group leader, J., that has not only helped me by showing me genuine care but is an example for me in the growth track. I believe that Jesus has something exciting in store for me to help others whose lives need to be changed. I am called for a higher purpose. ~MM

I WANT TO START by thanking the Lord, not only for what I have, but for the life He has given me. I will continue to use it until the day He calls me home. Before now, I didn't understand what a true relationship with the Lord feels like, but after having my eyes opened, I now know that it isn't something that only exists when you feel His presence but also when you don't. I had a habit of forming excuses as to why I shouldn't do what I'm called to, always forming a way to get out of the plan He has for me. I've realized that the only way to gain true happiness is to say yes to every door He opens. I no longer want to hide in the comfort of excuses. I want to say yes to going where He says to go. I want Him to guide me through life. I finally feel okay with not knowing what is ahead. It may be scary, but I know that with God there is no reason to be afraid. I feel called to kid's ministry or to work with a praise/worship team or maybe both. I want to fulfill whatever His plan is for me no matter what it is. I will lay down everything for him. ~TP

God is using me through the worship team to spread the gospel. He's blessed me with gifts of music along w/ the gift of tongues. I believe he has more for my life and will continue to open doors and reveal to me what my calling is.

God I pray that you develop my story. I thank you for a house, a family a school to minister to, a church, a youth group, a pastor, a sport, and everything else. God I thank you for everything.. help me figure out my calling and help me develop it. I feel god has called me to minister to my school.

MY ROAD TO LEADERSHIP!

God's Calling as Shared by Attendees at
CALLED CAMP/2025

I FEEL CALLED to youth ministry/mission field. I want to help teenagers get through their tough times in life. This season of life is challenging and hard, but God makes provision for every obstacle. As He has done it for me, I want teenagers to know He can do the same for them. ~BS

THANK YOU, GOD, for blessing me with my athletic abilities. Lord, I thank You for all the people who have planted in my life and for bringing me to Church of Hope. Thank You for helping me grow in my faith and helping me find my calling of whatever that might be. I ask that You help me to speak Your Word at school or wherever You are calling me. I thank You for Pastor C., J., and the other leaders who have poured into my life by helping me find the right path and leading me into student internship. It's helped me gain leadership by serving on the media team. Thank You, Lord, for never giving up on me. Whatever my calling is, I pray that You will lead me. ~WM

GOD HAS USED me in His work in many ways. I've served in the bursary and kid's church. But most of all God has used me to help others understand who God really is and how we should fear Him respectfully. ~OH

LORD, I THANK You for C. and those who have worked to provide this camp. I'm thankful for my friends and my mother as well. Ever since You've become a part of my life, things have changed for the better. I've been able to finally forgive my father and forgive those who have forsaken me. Now I want to experience everything You have for me. I pray that one day I will be able to share how You've helped me. I want You to be the center of my life and everything I do. You gave me peace in chaos. ~IC

I COME FROM a broken family. God wasn't in our lives, and although I grew up believing in God, I never surrendered to Him. I met my youth pastors, and they introduced me to God. I'm not sure what God is calling me to, but I know it is something exciting. ~B

I COME FROM a family who aren't really believers, and only my mom serves the Lord. In fact, she introduced me to church, where I met my youth pastor, B., J., and S. They've helped me grow in my relationship with Jesus. While I don't have confirmation of my specific calling, I know God is leading me. ~KG

I HAVE ALWAYS had an extreme sense of justice for what's fair and for what's right and/or wrong. Despite being raised a Christian, at times I felt there were shadows chasing me. I've had difficulty following the rules and therefore beat myself up and felt trapped with not being able to break the cycle. Then, I went to camp, and it changed my life. It set me back on track, and I felt my strong will and sense of justice now had a purpose. I feel that I am called to be a lawyer. I feel that it isn't fair that I've grown up knowing Jesus in a complete household and yet there are others who don't know Him. Perhaps I could practice law as a full-time missionary using my giftings and desires to serve the Lord and others. ~AT

ALL MY LIFE I've been a Christian, but on January 2, 2017, my life changed when my mom died of cancer. The following year my dad was involved in a horrible motorcycle accident, spending two months in a coma. I completely lost faith in God. I stopped going to church for four years. My sisters and my dad started attending church, so I went with them and met my amazing youth pastors. It was there that I met an old friend from elementary school and decided to attend church more often. I later went to summer camp and surrendered my life back to God and was baptized. Then I volunteered in VBS and taught kids about God. I attended Called Camp to explore my calling into ministry. ~JH

MY TESTIMONY IS difficult in that I am still trying to figure it all out. But what I do know is that I have grown up my whole life as a preacher's kid, at church all the time, and going to camp as much as possible. I never believed that You wanted me or called me, because I've gone through struggles and stuff. I want to feel Your presence and don't want to mess things up. ~CM

I AM CALLED to lead my generation and bring them back to Jesus. I am believing God for a generational revival, according to Acts 20:24. ~PD

MY STORY WAS traumatic for me because I had major family problems and failed relationships. My alcohol and drug abuse was a struggle, but I found the Lord and He changed everything. Now I follow Jesus! God has spoken to me to preach the good news to people that have yet to hear about Jesus. ~GM

I FEEL CALLED to be a missionary, because from the place I was in, I wouldn't have known if He hadn't sent someone to me. They told me how much God cared and loved me. I feel it is my duty to return the favor to those lost and without hope, those without Jesus. ~JF

MY CALLING IS to be an example to my family and to live a life running after God. I want to help others find the freedom I've found and bring in the lost. I want to show the love of God to hurting people. I am called to be a missionary, living a life of obedience and surrender. ~CB

Lord thank you for bringing me to called camp for the 2nd year! I cant even believe its been a year since I met you, and since you've placed these wonderful people in my life.

It wasn't by accident that Pheobe walked into my freshman spanish class because that moment is what changed my life Lord and has shown me that there is truly important meaning behind the experiences I have day to day. Lord you have given me eyes that see your beautiful creations on this earth and you have given me a heart and a mind that is eager and willing to hear and learn from you God. Although i'm still not clear on my calling from you God, you have taught me to trust you through the uncertanty.

God, a month ago I could barely play guitar and now I was able to write a song which is so crazy to me and the closest people to me love it. Lord I just ask that if that was a gift given from you, that you may help guide me into worship ministry in your timing Lord. God you are worthy of <u>my yes!</u> I ask that you seek my heart and my intentions God that you help me to find my identity, calling and passion in christ. <u>You are worthy of my surrender!</u>

No Holdbacks with God!

God's Calling as Shared by Attendees at
CALLED CAMP/2025

I GREW UP in church my whole life but struggled with so much that no one knew anything about. I could not get past the feeling that God couldn't want me, but I so desperately wanted freedom. He has now given me hope and saved me from my broken heart. I am convinced He is calling me to share His love and to evangelize and let people know that there is hope for them. ~SE

I GREW UP going to church. I was known as the youth pastor's daughter, which I hated. I tried so hard to prove that wasn't me, and that I didn't care about all of the sin in my life. Still, I wasn't happy. I was seeking world validation, and I fell into depression. After three years, I finally went to a hospital for my mental problems, but nothing seemed to have really changed. I started night school, thinking it's going to be a fresh start until one night, I was taken advantage of by a family member in the worst way. My self-esteem crumbled. I thought God had abandoned me, but then He came into my life. I now realize that my mom is a great example who has been leading me to teach the youth and show those who think they are alone that they have someone to talk to. I've helped girls in my church who were afraid to speak up. I have learned that my voice matters and that speaking with the words God gives me will change the world. ~An.

I ALWAYS PORTRAYED myself as the perfect little Christian girl, but it was only lies. I was baptized at age seven but knew it was fake. I didn't know what it meant to be God's child. By age nine or ten, I was involved in things that were dirty and disgusting. I went to church but felt empty. I wanted to change and at eleven, I was inducted into CORE. I needed to know whether the pastor could see something positive in me, because I felt dirty and useless. She encouraged me to worship, yet I didn't feel anything. How could my actions be worship? I eventually connected with God, but the memories never faded. I felt so stained. My family thought I was perfect, but I knew better. Now, I realize I am who I am, and I am ready to be used by God daily. I know that God uses the broken and makes them whole. ~AB

I TRULY DON'T even know where to begin. I first remember accepting Jesus as a young girl. From there, God always had my heart. I spoke in tongues for the first time at a kid's camp when I was nine or ten. Even though I was filled with the Spirit, I didn't habitually exercise my heavenly language with the Lord. I began to slowly fall away from Him. My seventh-grade year at a youth conference, I felt the Lord and Spirit in my heart while I was crying out to Him. It wasn't an audible voice, but it was definitely the Lord speaking to me. At the time, I was very far from the Lord and forgot what the Spirit was like, so the Lord had to remind me. I remember looking up at one of the stage lights and almost seeing an angel-like figure. Immediately I felt safe from the world. I felt set apart. In that moment, I felt that the Lord was calling me out of my sin and to something greater. After that, I had a "conference high" as people would call it, and I spent time with the Lord. Then life began to happen again. I went back to school into the eighth grade and began to fall back into sin. I was lying to my parents, cussing, and constantly being rude. I ended up having an incident my parents found out about. I lost their trust for a while, and it ended up making me rethink a lot about how I was acting and who I was surrounded by. After that, I really tried to improve. I stopped cussing and lying to my parents and ended a lot of friendships and relationships. I began to trust the Lord with my life. Going into ninth grade, I continued with the Lord but still felt so lost, lonely, confused, anxious, angry, and disrespectful. I felt like the Lord wasn't seeing me. One day, I decided to surrender it all to Him and trust Him ALWAYS! He brough me out of the lies of the enemy, out of loneliness, and He began to bring me Godly relationships to feed into me! He reminded me of the calling I have on my life. Ever since then I have tried to stay focused on Him and continue to make Him the foundation of my life. I've tried to continue to serve Him and spread His gospel to people who need His love and forgiveness. ~An.

THANK YOU, LORD, for everything You have done in my life and for everyone else as well. I want to start by saying, Lord, that maybe I haven't found what I am called to yet, but I know You will give me the courage and wellness to see the next step in my life. I know that whatever I'm called to do, You will help me, and I will have a called career with You. One day I'll be all grown up with a loving husband and maybe even a few kids, and still, I want to be called to something I am good at. I know You will lead me through the struggles I might go through. I love You so much and will forever cherish You in my life. Thank You, Jesus. You are the light of the world and a lamp unto my feet. ~An.

THANK YOU, LORD, that I am here. Thank You that I get to live a life of abundance because I know You. Thank You for Your grace and Your mercy that renews each day. I thank You that I had the privilege to know You at such a young age. I pray, Lord, that You light a fire in me that never runs out. Lord, I pray that You remove all anxiety, worry, self-doubt, and excuses that get in the way of what I am called to do. I want people to know You like I do. You are the center of it all. I humble myself before You and give You everything. Your way be done in my life. I surrender. I trust You with my whole heart, and I step aside for You to work and move in my life. You are the Author, my Abba, my Provider, King of kings, my Comforter, my Shield, my Rock. I lay it all down. Thank you, Lord, I adore You and Your wonders. Use me in ways I would never imagine. Your will be done. Amen.
~An.

WHEN I WAS younger, I always had the heart to give every penny I had for BGMC. I have that same motive with time now. Thank You, Lord, that I have the heart to push aside what I want in order to be there for Your people, the hurt, the lost, and the ones near me. You showed me true love and left the 99 so I'd be in Your arms. You set the example. You knew the things I'd do before I took my first breath. I've made so many mistakes, and You choose to love me anyway. I never wanted to be a missionary. I've always dreamed of having a huge house, a big family, lots of money, and a space in a nice area, but I felt that I could never accomplish that. When I first saw CALLED CAMP fliers for 2023, I was intrigued and wanted to go. I knew I was called to missions as a young girl, was so interested, and my heart hurt for those who suffered and didn't know you. Now I am choosing to lay down time, personal feelings, and wants to help others. ~JT

THANK YOU, LORD, for gifting me with breath in my lungs, the same breath that allows me to say yes to the call You have placed on my life. Long before I truly knew You as my savior, I knew that I was created for greater things. For my life's dream has always been to help those in need, to help those that don't have the means to receive the help they need. That not only will I be able to help but that I can lead and redirect people to You, Holy God. Often, all people need is You, for Your Holy Spirit to touch them and bring them out of whatever box the enemy has put them in. Lord God, I thank You for calling me to proclaim You as Lord to all around, for all that know me know that You are my Savior, my King, and my Lord. Those around me know that my greatest decision was to proclaim You as Lord over my life. ~An.

THANK YOU, THANK YOU for life, breath in my lungs, a heart for people, a family, friends, my education, my gifts and talents, thank You for everything You've given and will continue to give me. Guide me in my walk with You, guide me as a high schooler, as a sister, as a friend, even as a stranger. Use me as a vessel for Your honor and glory. Deepen my calling, increase my hunger, my thirst, my desire for You. Pour Your Spirit over me and my life. Give me dreams and visions. Your Word is a lamp unto my feet and a light unto my path. Shape me and mold me into who I need to be. Show me Your ways, Lord. Reveal my calling and gifts. You've given me and my family a calling as church planters. Use us, Lord, help us to reach the lost, help us to expand Your kingdom. Use me in my youth group, as I become a student leader. May You guide me to show Your love to others. Be with me in everything I do, so that I may not run away from You but to You. May I always go back to You when I am distracted, when I am doubtful, or when I am afraid. When I am lost, may I always look back to You. May I always run back to You. Thank You, Jesus, in Your mighty name I pray, amen. ~SP

THANK YOU, LORD, for the opportunities You have given me ... the ability to love on the babies in the nursery, showing them a glimpse of Your love at a young age when they don't really know words yet. I know that part of my story and calling has something to do with kids. Lord, I thank You for the amazing people You have placed in my life. Thank You for giving them to me to help me on my path. I'm not too sure where it's going, but You do. You have spoken to them, so they can speak to me. You knew that I would need people to reassure me that You have a plan for me, one that will honor You. Help me to fulfill it and not be scared of the unknown. Give me peace of mind. Help me to live in the uncomfortable seasons. Lord, I want to live out the plan You have for me at the fullest, with no holdbacks, nothing. Lord, whatever You are calling me to, show me. Show me where You want me and what You have in store for me. Open my eyes to see, Lord. I know You want me to minister to others. I know that for sure. But I'm just not sure how. So, over this weekend, show me the plans You have for me. I know You are going to bring me places that need Your love. I believe You are going to send me around the world spreading Your gospel where they don't even know You yet. I thank You for the calling You have on my life. ~M

I AM CALLED!

I stood behind the podium, looking over the heads of a couple hundred students who were ready to hear God's Word, and for a moment I was transported back in time. There, just about 30 yards from where I stood in January of 2023, was the place where in June of 1991 I finally surrendered to the call of God on my life to ministry. I remember it so clearly...

After being called to preach at the age of fifteen during an all-night prayer meeting for the healing of a man in our church who had leukemia, I walked away from my relationship with the Lord several months later. Not long after that, I abandoned the call of God on my life to ministry. I wouldn't come back to the Lord until I was twenty, and when I did come back, like the prodigal son,

I was full of shame and regret. I knew the Lord had forgiven me, and I was so grateful for His mercy and grace, but I did not believe He would ever want to use me in ministry. I determined to serve Him and those He WOULD use in ministry.

So when my youth pastor invited me to take a couple days off from work to come help him lead worship at a youth camp in the summer of '91, I gladly obliged. I thought I was going to help him and serve other students. Little did I know that God had plans for me that week.

One night during the altar time of that youth camp, we found ourselves back on the low platform of the open-air tabernacle there in Kerrville, Texas. A couple of the ceiling fans were missing blades, and the remaining ones drooped. There were musty carpet remnants on the dusty concrete in front of heavy wooden altars that had more coats of paint on them than seemed possible. But none of that kept the Holy Spirit from moving in the lives of those present. There were students across the front, slain under the power of the Holy Spirit. There were students and youth leaders doing a Jericho march (Google it) around the perimeter of the Tabernacle. And we were singing, worshiping God from the depths of our souls.

I sensed the presence of the Lord so strongly that I stepped behind the screen that the overhead projector (ask ChatGPT) shone the words on. In that moment, I sensed the Lord say to me, "Allen, I still want you to preach."

I argued, "But God, You don't want me. I've messed up too much. How could You ever use me?"

Just like He didn't accept Moses' excuses, He didn't accept mine. And just like the father instructed his servants about the prodigal son who had returned, the Lord graciously restored me. He said, "Allen, I still want you."

In that moment, I made my decision. I told the Lord, "If you'll take me back for ministry, then I will go anywhere You want me to go, say anything You want me to say, and do anything You want me to do, as long as You're going to call the shots."

And in that moment, He said, "Let's go!"

Suddenly I was back in the much nicer auditorium of that same campground, standing in front of students waiting to hear the Word. Thirty years had passed. Three decades that included serving in a variety of ministry roles and assignments. And that night, my assignment was to give another generation of students the opportunity to answer that same call to ministry.

Something happened that January weekend. I remember Pastor Tim Barker, our Network Superintendent, saying, "This can't just be an annual event. It has to be more. We have to do more with these students to help them pursue the call of God on their lives."

I couldn't get away from it. As the CALLED team began to dream, we began to believe God has much more in store for us to help these young people become all God intends them to become and accomplish all the dreams for ministry that God has placed inside them. But I also couldn't get away from the truth that the call of God on my own life is just as alive and vibrant today as it was when I finally said "Yes" to God. In fact, He is birthing more dreams for ministry in my heart, and I am energized to not only serve in ministry myself, but also to help others pursue the dreams God has placed in their hearts.

My name is Allen Chapin, and I am CALLED. "Let's go!"

Notes

Notes

Notes

Notes

www.ingramcontent.com/pod-product-compliance
Lightning Source LLC
Chambersburg PA
CBHW052114090426

42741CB00009B/1801